SOME OBSERVATIONS
ON THE
ART OF NARRATIVE

THE MACMILLAN COMPANY
NEW YORK · BOSTON · CHICAGO
DALLAS · ATLANTA · SAN FRANCISCO

MACMILLAN AND CO., LIMITED
LONDON · BOMBAY · CALCUTTA
MADRAS · MELBOURNE

**THE MACMILLAN COMPANY
OF CANADA, LIMITED**
TORONTO

SOME OBSERVATIONS
ON THE
ART OF NARRATIVE

BY

PHYLLIS BENTLEY

NEW YORK

THE MACMILLAN COMPANY

1947

CONTENTS

SOME OBSERVATIONS
ON THE
ART OF NARRATIVE

I

INTRODUCTION

"AN ARTIST," writes Arnold Bennett (*Journals, Vol. I*), "must be interested primarily in presentment, not in the thing presented. He must have a passion for technique, a deep love for form." On the other hand, W. Somerset Maugham (*The Summing-up*) remarks: "The artist is absorbed by his technique only when his theme is of no pressing interest to him."

These two truths are not necessarily incompatible. The expert tennis player, when called on to deal during a match with a tennis ball bouncing in a remote corner of the court, does not consciously consider the technique of foot and wrist necessary to reach and hit the white sphere in the available number of seconds before, with its present speed and angle, it falls to earth. In a practice game he might thus consciously reflect, but in a match he simply leaps across the ground and turning his wrist delivers a swift and well-placed backhand stroke. If he thought consciously he would lack the time to act. But it is owing to previous training of foot and hand, to long, conscious and careful study and practice of his technique, that at the moment of action all these considerations are fused into a perfectly co-ordinated movement of the muscles. He thinks about winning the point, not about his left foot, but only long footwork study enables him to leave his left foot with impunity to look after itself. Of course, there are players of such genius that no study is necessary; but the young player is well advised not to consider himself of their number. Of course, too, tennis players play tennis because they are passionately interested in that particular method of muscular activity.

All this is a commonplace in games and in most arts. Sculptors are presumed to find it necessary to learn how to model clay and handle a chisel before they try to express some profound thought about the origins of life in marble. Painters study anatomy and colour. Composers know the structure of the scale. Poets are usually familiar with the rhyme schemes of the sonnet before trying to compose one. Certainly all critics of these arts are required to be well versed in their technique. In any case, if practitioners and critics are not familiar with these techniques, it is their own fault, since colours, notes and scansions have been clearly defined and the definitions copiously discussed and recorded.

In the art of fiction it is not so. The *corpus* of fiction criticism is small and on the whole lightly regarded, compared with that of other arts, and such criticism as exists deals almost entirely with the material or the pattern rather than with the actual fabric of fiction. Few critiques exist on general fiction topics comparable with those on the æsthetics and mechanics of drama and poetry. Many books have been written to discuss the achievements of individual novelists, which cite and praise his characters, his story, his scene, even his style, but few mention his actual method of presentation, his narrative. It is as if books were written about all the bodies painted by

Michelangelo, stating and praising their varied flesh tints, rosy, sallow or bronze, but never mentioning the actual application of paint by which these tints were achieved. The famous prefaces of Henry James describe in gloriously minute detail the master's materials and his design, the pattern in his carpet and the coloured woods of which it is to be woven; but only rarely do they touch on the actual process of weaving. Percy Lubbock alone, in *The Craft of Fiction*, has attempted an analysis of fiction narrative, and that brilliant work, though a classic of fiction criticism, is obstructed in its pursuit of truth, in my view, by a mistaken terminology. Indeed ignorance on the subject of fiction narrative prevails to such an extent that its terminology is as yet quite undetermined—unlike the novel's young cousin the film, where the *frame*, the *shot* and the *sequence* convey definite ideas. Recent attacks on, recent divergencies from, the traditional type of fiction narrative, seem to me therefore to have proceeded from false premises though often empirically useful.

As a practitioner rather than a critic, I venture to offer a few observations on the art of narrative in fiction, in the hope that they may indicate the scope of the territory to be covered by future fiction criticism, and the problems to be solved.

II

TYPES OF NARRATIVE

I FIND I can explain my view of the nature of narrative in fiction, its varieties and the place it occupies between the reader and the imaginary world of the novel most easily if I translate a psychological fact into a physical metaphor, and say that the reader is divided from the imaginary world of the novel by a high wall over which he cannot see. On the top of the wall is perched the novelist. He looks down into the world of his imagination and then turns to the reader and tells him what is going on there. The novelist does not, like the dramatist, pick up bits of his world and set them down on the near side of the wall for actors to animate and his audience to see; the novelist narrates; he tells what he sees.

What is it that he sees? The world of the particular novel which is at present engaging him; a tremendous three-dimensional pageant of life, not endless, but rolling continuously past the novelist's mental eye. A seething flux of phenomena, continually changing, continually transmuting as to some of its items, continually rolling, sweeping, surging, sparking and banging by.

Since this world, this moving pageant, is the novelist's creation, he is of course omniscient and omnipotent with regard to it.

4

He is omniscient—the cries of its birds, the thuds of its battles, the thoughts of its people, its clouds, its sunsets, its leaves, its deepest emotions and vastest plains, are all part of its seething flux and he knows them all.

He is omnipotent—he can alter his pageant at will, he can survey any part, in any way, at will. He can look at it or not look at it, as he likes, whenever he likes. He can look at parts of it and not at other parts, if he likes. He can hold it at a distance, he can draw it close. He has its progress, its rolling, completely under his control; he can make it go past him swiftly or slowly, as he likes; he can reverse it backwards, and bring it up again with a jerk, if he chooses. And he does so choose; he delights in handling his pageant variously. Before he begins to tell about his pageant to his readers, he has rolled it backwards and forwards many a score of times, trying to improve its interest and its beauty, trying, too, to decide how he shall handle it on that final occasion when he tells it to his readers.

There are as many ways of rolling a pageant as there are human minds, but in our metaphor the speed of the process is the operative factor in the type of narrative we receive. Sometimes the novelist rolls the pageant by swiftly, so swiftly that details are not discernible. Sometimes the novelist rolls it slowly, so that he sees (and tells) each specific action, hears each actual word. Sometimes he halts it altogether for a moment.

Suppose, for example, a part of the novelist's imaginary world concerns the journey of his hero Dick and his villain Tom from a village in Central Africa to London. The rolling pageant brings in its course Dick and Tom to a long stretch of desert. The desert (this is in Victorian times) is all the same and not very important, and so the novelist rolls it swiftly by. He does *not* say: "Dick and Tom raised their right foot and put it down, striding over a yard of sand, and then raised their left foot and put it down, striding over another yard of sand," and go on saying that or something like it until Tom and Dick have marched two hundred miles, and at last reach a palm tree. At the same time he is bound to give an impression of the two hundred miles, for the remoteness, the loneliness, of Dick and Tom is highly important. He therefore holds his pageant at a distance so that he can see its full breadth and rolls it quickly by; he tells us in a few paragraphs about the distant mountains, the burning sun, the sand, the heat of the day, how the feelings of loneliness of Dick and Tom heightened with the journey, and so on. Then when he has created a sufficient impression of the vast stretch of desert lying between the travellers and civilisation, he goes on:

The sun was just sinking as Dick and Tom entered the Zazifa oasis.

Something important in his story is going to happen in this oasis, he knows; so he slows up the pageant, and looks very intently at this one portion of it. Now that it is going so slowly, instead of a blur of sound he can hear voices, instead of a white blank he can see the nose and eyes and cheeks of a face, instead of a pulsating ribbon of cerebration he can perceive the thoughts of Dick and Tom at this single moment. And so, instead of telling us summaries of speech and personality and behaviour, he tells us specific words and actions. We read his account of the exact words in which Dick and Tom quarrel, the exact knife-blow with which Tom murders Dick, the exact thoughts, horrified yet rejoicing, with which Tom buries the body.

But the rest of Tom's journey to England isn't important in the least, so the novelist simply declines to look at it; he whizzes it by in a flash, so fast that he does not see it at all. He ends his chapter, that is to say; he breaks off his narrative, begins it again only when the liner carrying Tom approaches Southampton. Tom's landing in England isn't very important, so we have a fairly swift narrative of the disembarkation—with one slower view perhaps at the bookstall, where Tom sees an account of Dick's death in a travel magazine. The pageant rolls by fairly swiftly as Tom travels up to London—we must have an impression of farms and green fields, to convey that this is civilisation, but do not need to travel the journey mile by mile.

But now Tom arrives at the London terminus, and is met by Ellen, the girl to whom Dick was engaged, the girl whom Tom hopes to marry. This meeting is of the first importance. The novelist therefore slows up the pageant and takes a long slow look, and tells us everything that happened in minute detail—Tom's struggles to play a part in look and word, Ellen's candid grief presently becoming shadowed by distrust.

When the novelist halts his moving world and tells us what he sees, we term that type of narrative a *description*. When he moves it slowly and tells us single specific actions (including of course those specific actions we call speech and thought), we have learned to term that type of narrative a *scene*. When he rolls his fictitious world by rapidly, so that he gives us, not each specific moment

7

of many battles but the integrated campaign, not the single impressions of a character but the sum of that character, not the minute by minute thoughts of a man but a summarised account of his gradual conversion to a new course of life—what is the term for that type of narration? Unfortunately there is no generally accepted term. Percy Lubbock calls these summaries *retrospect* when they refer to the past, but that covers only one of their functions. I myself have adopted the term *summary* to express these condensations, these integrations, but I am not at all satisfied with it. The words *scene* and *summary*, *description* and *summary*, are not proper antitheses. Though indeed—and this is the crux of the argument— the kinds of narrative described above are not antitheses, but distant points in a scale of subtle gradations, stretching from the specific to the integrated.

For all narrative is in fact a summary to some degree. The most specific scene does not narrate the contraction of the muscles, the rush of the impulse along the grey ganglions of the mind, which produces speech or smile. When Virginia Woolf, devotee of the specific, writes: "Thick wax candles stand upright; young men rise in white gowns; while the subservient eagle bears up for inspection the great white book" (*Jacob's Room*), she is summarising the complex interactions of systems of internal stresses subjected to external forces, the involved activity of muscular tissue, which makes the candles hold upright in their sconces, the book rest on the eagle, the young men rise. Kipling in his short story *The Ship that Found Herself* specificised (if the word may be forgiven) the movement of a ship; but to state: "a steel girder quivered" is still to summarise the play of conflicting

8

tensions. James Joyce records the swift succession of thought association, but even he does not detail the physical nerve processes of which they are a result. Still, for practical purposes the place on the scale of the specific of the scene and the summary are sufficiently far apart to justify different names.

The metaphor of the wall and the rolling pageant is a metaphor only, and metaphors though often illuminating are in the last resort untrue, being metaphors and not the thing itself. The story of Dick and Tom and Ellen was a crude invented instance. The truth or falsity of the suggested definition of scene and summary must be tested in the actual narratives of fiction.

III

USE OF SUMMARY

THE scene and the summary have quite distinct uses, distinct parts to play, in fiction. The place of the summary is very well explained by Fielding in *Tom Jones:*

We intend in it (the novel) rather to pursue the method of those writers who profess to disclose the revolutions of countries, than to imitate the painful and voluminous historian, who, to preserve the regularity of his series, thinks himself obliged to fill up as much paper with the details of months and years in which nothing remarkable happened, as he employs upon those notable eras when the greatest scenes have been transacted on the human stage. Such histories as these do in reality very much resemble a newspaper, which consists of just the same number of words, whether there be any news in it or not . . .

Now it is our purpose in the ensuing pages to pursue a contrary method: when any extraordinary scene presents itself, as we trust will often be the case, we shall spare no pains nor paper to open it at large to our reader; but if whole years should pass without producing any thing worthy of his notice, we shall not be afraid of a chasm in our history, but shall hasten on to matters of consequence. . . .

(Book II, chapter i.)

Good writers will, indeed, do well to imitate the ingenious

traveller . . . who always proportions his stay at any place
to the beauties, elegancies, and curiosities which it affords.
(Book XI, chapter ix.)

That is to say, when the novelist requires to traverse
rapidly large tracts of the world of the novel which are
necessary to the story, but not worth dwelling long upon
—not worth narrating in the specific detail of a scene—
the summary is what he uses. For example:

We lived in an uninterrupted course of ease and content
for five years . . .
(Defoe: *Moll Flanders.*)

They travelled as expeditiously as possible; and, sleeping
one night on the road, reached Longbourn by dinner-time
the next day.
(Jane Austen: *Pride and Prejudice*, Ch. 47.)

Elizabeth passed the chief of the night in her sister's room.
(Jane Austen: *Pride and Prejudice*, Ch. 9.)

In the course of the day I was enrolled a member of the
fourth class, and regular tasks and occupations were assigned
me.
(Charlotte Brontë: *Jane Eyre*, ch. vi.)

Mr. Dick and I soon became the best of friends.
In less than a fortnight I was quite at home, and happy,
amongst my new companions.
(Charles Dickens: *David Copperfield*, ch. xv.)

She had been led through the best galleries, had been
taken to the chief points of view, had been shown the grand-
est ruins and the most glorious churches . . .
(George Eliot: *Middlemarch*, ch. 20.)

Some months of homely courtship ensued.

> (Meredith: *The Egoist*, ch. iii.)

The news became known in trading circles throughout the town.

> (Arnold Bennett: *The Old Wives' Tale*, ch. iv.)

Sir Francis's career had not come up to his expectations.
> (Virginia Woolf: *Night and Day*.)

Mary spent her first week in London very quietly. She visited a few shops, but for the most part she stayed in (her) rooms, and read, or thought of John. . . . At the end of a week she wanted action. She ordered herself a plum-coloured habit and hired a horse and a groom to ride with her in the Park.

> (Storm Jameson: *The Lovely Ship*.)

Note how in that last passage the summary goes down the sliding scale of specificity towards the scene. The first two sentences are highly condensed summary, the third sentence is less so. In the fourth sentence we receive such specific details as the colour of the habit and the ordering of a groom, though we are not told the incidents in which Mary orders and buys them. The following sentence beings: "The morning of her first ride was cold"—a specific time is established, and we glide off into a scene, where Mary rides in the Park, has her horse disturbed by a hat scudding between his feet, receives the apologies of the young man who owns the hat, and so on.

The summary is particularly useful, too, when a whole way of life is to be indicated as a background to the main characters' specific activities. There are some fine passages of summary of this kind in Thackeray's chapter "How to

12

Live Well on Nothing a Year" in *Vanity Fair*. To have told all the activities summarised there in specific action would have occupied infinitely more space and labour than they were worth to the story. A neat example of a social summary occurs in Galsworthy's *The Man of Property*:

> They had all done so well for themselves, these Forsytes, that they were all what is called "of a certain position." They had shares in all sorts of things, not as yet in consols, for they had no dread in life like that of 3 per cent. for their money. They collected pictures, too, and were supporters of such charitable institutions as might be beneficial to their sick domestics . . .
>
> (Galsworthy: *The Man of Property*, Ch. i.)

One of the most important and frequent uses of the summary is to convey rapidly a stretch of *past* life. The novelist, having excited our interest in his characters by telling a scene to us, suddenly whizzes his pageant back, then forward, giving us a rapid summary of their past history, a retrospect. Percy Lubbock has discussed the theory and practice of the retrospect with such penetration and such erudition that it would be idle to enter deeply into the subject here, but one or two examples of fine retrospects may be interesting. In *Clayhanger* Edwin sees a tear on the cheek of an old Sunday-school teacher. The tear is explained (Chapter iv) by a retrospective summary, some twelve pages long, which sums up the whole of the life of Edwin's father—and the whole of the life of pottery operatives in the early 19th century as well. Trollope's retrospective summary of the tragic history of Mary's birth in *Dr. Thorne* is famous for its vitality and interest, though somewhat overlong. An amusingly laconic summary, of which the brevity forms the bite, is Aldous Huxley's account of the course of the intrigue between Walter Bidlake and Marjorie Carling, which occupies eight lines of the first page of *Point Counterpoint*.

The summary if unskilfully handled can become exceedingly tedious. "What is the use of a book without pictures or conversations?" thought Alice just before the White Rabbit ran by, in condemnation of the book her sister was reading, and this childish comment is supported by novel-readers of all degrees of intelligence. Long close paragraphs of print are in themselves apt to dismay the less serious readers and their instinct here is a sound one, for an excess of summary and an insufficiency of scene in a novel makes the story seem remote, without bite, second-hand; for in a summary the novelist is selecting, so to speak, from his own selection; we feel we might have summarised differently if we had seen more fully. Besides, the summary tends to throw the events summarised into the past; we feel that they must have happened long ago or time would have lacked for the process of summarising.

Possibly the worst example in good English fiction of the misuse of summary occurs at the beginning of *Waverley*. Omitting chapter one, which discusses the kind of story Scott intends to write, as not really part of the novel, we begin chapter two by a somewhat indirect but specific statement that sixty years ago Edward Waverley took leave of his family to join a regiment of dragoons in which he had lately obtained a commission, and that it was a melancholy day at Waverley-Honour when the young officer parted with Sir Everard, his uncle. This is a hopeful start; for the sake of the battles and adventures it seems to promise, most readers would be perfectly willing to tackle a few paragraphs, or even a few pages, of retrospective summary explaining who the two Waverleys are, with their respective situations. But Scott gives us four chapters of summary without a single scene. Not until the opening of chapter six do we leave retrospect and come to: "It was upon the evening of this memorable Sunday that Sir Everard entered the library. . . ." It is a specific action; at last we are being given a scene, where the kind of action we call speech is soon vouchsafed to us. The naïve monotony, the stale second-hand air, of an unbroken summary, four chapters long, would be intolerable to the sophisticated modern reader.

The placing and introduction of the summary is a matter requiring great skill. Perhaps I may be forgiven if I cite a personal instance of bad placing. In a novel of mine called *The Spinner of the Years*, a family, the Armitages, are sitting at dinner when the bell rings; the son of the house goes out to see who has arrived, and returns, bringing with him a young lad, Johnnie Talland. At this point I broke off, and gave eight pages of retrospective summary, covering Johnnie's career since the Armitages last saw him. When the novel was published a critic complained of this. The criticism vexed me, for it was clear that the critic knew nothing about the art of narrative, he had no idea that all summary occurred between two scenes. But in fact the critic, though less well informed in the technique of fiction, had a sounder story-telling instinct than I, for the summary was undoubtedly ill-placed. I had not sufficiently excited the readers' curiosity about Johnnie to make them want a summary about him; all they were eager about at the moment was what the young Imogen Armitage, upon whom interest had been concentrated, felt at the meeting. A few more sentences, an uncertainty in Johnnie's manner which hinted an inconvenience in his life, would have reconciled the reader to a summary which satisfied his curiosity.

The transition from one kind of narrative to another is also a ticklish job. It can be done in the baldest crudest way, as when Defoe (*Moll Flanders*) in the middle of a scene breaks into summary by remarking: "Here he gave me a long history of his life, which indeed would make a very strange history, and be infinitely diverting. He told me . . ." or George Eliot begins a chapter of retrospective summary on Tertius Lydgate's career by announcing with equal frankness: "At present I have to make the new settler Lydgate better known to anyone interested in him. . . ." (*Middlemarch*). But other novelists, whether of the 18th, 19th or 20th century, show such an infinite subtlety in making their transitions that a very pointed tool is necessary to disentangle the interweavings. A great part of the vigour, the vivacity and the readability of Dickens derives from his innumerable interweavings of scene and summary; his general method is to keep summary to the barest essential minimum, a mere sentence or two here and there between the incredibly fertile burgeoning of his scenes. Thus the fabric of his narrative remains always very closely woven.

The later novelists, too, employ endless devices to make summary appear as scene and thus rob it of its tedium, casting it in the guise of one character's reflections upon another, dialogue between two characters, and so on. But of the contemporary disrepute of summary I shall speak later.

IV

USE OF SCENE

It will not be necessary to furnish many examples of
scenes from fiction, since the whole weight of fiction
criticism hitherto seems directed upon nothing else. Here
are a few short examples, extracts from narrative scenes
in well-known novels. To avoid confusing the issue, I
have chosen several passages which are not "scenes" in
the violent sense of the word.

Upon opening the clothes, to his great surprise he beheld
an infant wrapped up in some coarse linen, in a sweet and
profound slumber, between his sheets.

(Fielding: *Tom Jones*.)

Mr. Darcy smiled; but Elizabeth thought she could perceive that he was rather offended, and therefore checked her
laugh.

(Jane Austen: *Pride and Prejudice*.)

All at once, without speaking, he struck suddenly and
strongly. I tottered, and on regaining my equilibrium retired
back a step or two from his chair.

(Charlotte Brontë: *Jane Eyre*.)

"When will you see her?" said the signora with a start.
"See whom?" said the bishop.

"My child," said the mother.

"What is the young lady's age?" asked the bishop.

"She is just seven," said the signora.

"Oh," said the bishop, shaking his head: "She is much too young—very much too young."

(Trollope: Barchester Towers.)

The card of Lieutenant Patterne was handed to Sir Willoughby, who laid it on the salver, saying to the footman: "Not at home."

(Meredith: The Egoist.)

Mrs. Durrant sat in the drawing-room by a lamp winding a ball of wool. Mr. Clutterbuck read *The Times*. In the distance stood a second lamp, and round it sat the young ladies, flashing scissors. . . . Mr. Wortley read a book.

"Yes; he is perfectly right," said Mrs. Durrant, drawing herself up and ceasing to wind her wool.

(Virginia Woolf: Jacob's Room.)

In all the above passages, specific actions are narrated: the characters see, speak, strike, smile, think, kneel, read, push, wind wool; a card is handed, scissors flash.

The scene gives the reader a feeling of participating in the action very intensely, for he is hearing about it contemporaneously, exactly as it occurs and the moment it has occurred; the only interval between its occuring and the reader hearing about it is that occupied by the novelist's voice telling it. The scene is therefore used for intense moments. The crisis, the climax, of a sequence of actions is always (by novelists who know their craft) narrated in scene. When Darcy proposes to Elizabeth, when Rochester's wedding to Jane is interrupted; when Micawber reveals Uriah Heep's wickedness, when Paul

Dombey dies; when Rawdon discovers Becky's unfaithfulness with Lord Steyne, when Constance Baines hurls Mr. Povey's tooth from the window; when Ferrand talks about English hypocrisy to Dick Shelton, when Aziz undergoes his trial for assault, when Jess Oakroyd tears up his insurance card—whenever an important action occurs, whenever an important decision is taken—it is presented in scene. The Victorian novelists, however, did not waste full-dress scenes on minor incidents. Dickens with his light touch, his agile grace, is in and out of a minor scene in a couple of sentences; the heavier-handed write fewer and longer scenes, fewer and longer summaries.

It is not possible to convey the same *amount*, the same *volume* of information in a scene as in a summary of the same length, but by a highly significant or symbolic scene an equally valid impression of the portion of life being presented may be created. (Some would say a more valid, a more truthful, as well as a more vivid, impression.) The difference in method is between loading a single incident with significance or taking the essence of many incidents, between offering some terms to represent the mathematical series, or offering the summation of the whole; between selection and integration.

The scene method alone cannot give an extensive background, cannot give a long stretch of past history, cannot give explanations—at least, it can do so only by employing a great number of scenes, thus wasting the reader's time and attention, and throwing the story out of proportion. Percy Lubbock makes the interesting point that in *Anna Karenina* Tolstoy destroys one of his finest effects by not using summary (which Lubbock calls retrospect) sufficiently. Anna renounces her world for love—but Tolstoy never gives us a panorama of her glittering social world through summary, he employs scenes alone. These scenes, concludes Lubbock, are not numerous enough or significant enough to give an impression of St. Petersburg society against which Anna's later loneliness would stand out strongly. Few would cavil at any method employed in a novel so essentially satisfying as *Anna Karenina*, but there are many instances (I believe) in modern novels where a greater use of summary would have improved the work. In Virginia Woolf's *The Years*, for example, where the fortunes of the Pargiter family from 1880 to 1937 are presented in scenes only, we are conscious of great gaps in our knowledge of the family, for lack of linking and explanatory summary. We are conscious too, I think, of tedium in the constant re-establishing of time and place. North Pargiter complains that he is always finding himself on another strange doorstep, and the great difficulty of the "maximum scene" method is that somehow or other the location, type and ownership of the fresh doorstep has every time to be indicated. The modern novelist enjoys making these locations in subtle and indirect fashion, but in his efforts to avoid the crudity and monotony of repeated direct statements his subtlety sometimes becomes obscurity and the reader is involved in a guessing competition.

The scene is undoubtedly the most important, the most significant and the most entertaining of the novelist's available types of narrative. But it is not the only type.

V

ART OF NARRATIVE

THE proper use, the right mingling, of scene, description and summary is the art of fictitious narrative.

It is difficult to give many examples without over-weighting this text with slabs of quotations involving whole pages of fiction, so perhaps I may be allowed to give the text of one brief passage only, to illustrate the method of analysis, and then analyse the opening pages of *Vanity Fair*, as an example to serve as typical of many.

Description: The moon was set, and it was very dark;
Scene: Bessie carried a lantern, whose light glanced on wet steps and gravel road . . .

Description: Raw and chill was the winter morning;
Scene: My teeth chattered as I hastened down the drive. . . . The distant roll of the wheels announced the coming coach; I went to the door and watched its lamps approach rapidly through the gloom. . . . The coach drew up . . . my trunk was hoisted up; I was taken from Bessie's neck, to which I clung with kisses. "Be sure and take good care of her!" cried she to the guard. "Ay, ay!" was the answer; the door was slapped to, and on we drove.

Summary:	We appeared to travel over hundreds of
	miles. . . . We passed through several towns,
Scene:	and in one, a very large one, the coach
	stopped; the horses were taken out, and the
	passengers alighted to dine. I was carried
	into an inn. . . .

(Charlotte Brontë: Jane Eyre.)

The close interweaving of the types of narrative in that short passage may be noted as typical. Let us now analyse a more extended piece, from a master hand.

Vanity Fair opens thus:

While the present century was in its teens, and on one sunshiny morning in June, there drove up to the great iron gate of Miss Pinkerton's Academy for young ladies, on Chiswick Mall, a large family coach . . .

"There drove up a coach"—we are being told of a specific action at a specific time in a specific place; that is a scene. The scene continues for three or four pages; Miss Jemima Pinkerton sees the coach, comments on it to her sister; they talk; in their talk it transpires that Amelia Sedley is leaving the Academy that day and that another pupil, Becky Sharp, is accompanying her. Miss Pinkerton inscribes a farewell copy of Johnson's Dictionary for Amelia, declines Jemima's request to inscribe one for Becky Sharp. Then Thackeray glides off into a mingled summary and description, telling us what Amelia was like and certain passages of her past history. This takes a couple of pages. Then (page 6) we hear: "The hour of parting came." Miss Pinkerton and Amelia part (summary gliding into the specific); Miss Pinkerton and

Becky part (definitely scene—Becky makes her farewells in French which her schoolmistress does not understand); there is a rapid account of the parting with the pupils; the two girls enter Amelia's coach (scene); Jemima hands in some sandwiches and a copy of the Dictionary for Becky, though uninscribed (scene); Becky throws the Dictionary out of the window (scene); the carriage rolls away and the gates are closed (scene), and chapter one is over.

Chapter two begins with a scene between Amelia and Becky in the coach; then Thackeray goes into a four-page retrospect, chiefly summary mingled with a little short scene here and there, telling us Becky's past.

Many a dun had she talked to, and turned away from her father's door; many a tradesman had she coaxed and wheedled into good-humour . . . The rigid formality of the place suffocated her . . . She had not been much of a dissembler, until now her loneliness taught her to feign . . .

When Thackeray has finished summarising Becky's past, he glides into scene:

When at length home was reached, Miss Amelia Sedley skipped out on Sambo's arm. . . . She showed Rebecca over every room in the house. . . . She insisted upon Rebecca accepting the white cornelian . . . she determined in her heart to ask her mother's permission to present her white Cashmere shawl to her friend.

The white Cashmere shawl had been brought home from India by Amelia's brother Joseph, and the scene continues and becomes even more specific as Amelia and

Sedley talk about Joseph. The dinner-bell rings and the two girls go down to dinner (scene) and the chapter ends.

Chapter three begins with a scene between the girls and Joseph, then goes off into a retrospective summary about Joseph Sedley.

His bulk caused Joseph much anxious thought and alarm. Now and again he would make a desperate attempt to get rid of his superabundant fat; but his indolence and love of good living speedily got the better of these endeavours at reform. . . . He took the hugest pains to adorn his big person and passed many hours daily in that occupation. . . .

If we were given an account of one specific occasion when Joseph at a specific time and place stood before his mirror dressing for hours, that would be a scene; but Thackeray rightly judged that the Collector of Boggley Wallah at his dressing-table was not worth so long pausing over, and summarises him in a page and a half. But Joseph taking Becky in to dinner, and Becky's attempts to capture his interest, are worth a scene and get one which lasts till the end of the chapter.

Downstairs, then, they went, Joseph very red and blushing, Rebecca very modest, and holding her green eyes downwards. . . . I must be quiet, thought Rebecca, and very much interested about India.

Chapter four begins with a brief summary:

Poor Joe's panic lasted for two or three days. . . . As for Mr. Sedley's jokes, Rebecca laughed at them with a cordiality and perseverance. . . .

And so on for two paragraphs. Then:

Once, in looking over some drawings which Amelia had sent from school, Rebecca came upon one which caused her to burst into tears and leave the room.

This is scene again.

And so it goes on through this and every other English novel written between 1719 and 1919: scene, summary, description, scene, summary. The blend of scene, summary and description is—or was between 1719 and 1919 (Defoe and Woolf)—the novelist's medium, his fictitious prose narrative; through and by this he must present his material; through and by this he must portray characters and actions representative of reality in a plot of more or less complexity; through and by this he must give us that impression of dynamic life which is the purpose of all art.

What are the powers and the limitations of this medium?

VI

THE prose narrative of the novel has only one limitation: it is confined to words. The novelist cannot show you the actual colour of his heroine's eyes and curls, of the trees in the woods, of the heather on the moors, as a painter (or a technicolor film) can. He cannot show you actual shapes, as a sculptor can. He cannot let you hear an actual lark's song, actual thunder, actual voices—as a play, a film, a radio-play can. The novelist cannot give his readers real trees, or painted trees, or marble trees, or wooden trees or photographs of trees, or let you hear the sound of the trees; he can only give you trees in words.

VII

ITS POWERS

BUT IT IS these words which enable him to blend scene and description with summary; it is these words, therefore, which enable the novelist to present life with such unique and astonishing power. For not only is the novelist able to compress longer stretches of time, vaster stretches of space, into his work than any other kind of artist. His dual command of the specific and the integrated enables him to present *change*, change either slow or rapid, with an ease and power no other art form possesses.

Consider, for example, what tremendous scope his narrative allows him in his setting, that continuum of time and place in which his characters move.

His medium gives him the maximum freedom with regard to place. In a novel the reader can be offered as many landscapes as the novelist wishes, and these landscapes may be as large, as small, as different and as distant, as he desires. He can command landscapes inside the house, the palace, the church, and furnish them as he pleases; he can command landscapes of Alps, tundras, glaciers, a shoreless sea, a bird's nest, a boat on Yarmouth sands, a boudoir, a battlefield, or the Brighton Road. His background may be a moving object such as a train, a coach, an aeroplane; it may include a flying-bomb or a rocket, an army moving over acres of ground to battle, a fleet in action.

To obtain an authentic sample of the scope of background change in fiction, I once listed the landscapes in a novel of my own (*Inheritance*). I counted thirteen houses, six mills, five inns, three stations, two trains, a Cloth Hall, a Public Library, a Castle, a church, a post office, a Co-operative Society's lecture room and a bank, besides moors, roads, lanes, hills, bridges and streets innumerable. I found, too, that the story moved continually back and forth between these settings; I counted the changes of background up to one hundred and fifty and then finding myself not yet half-way through the book desisted, believing my point sufficiently proved. In a really large-scale novel, such as *War and Peace*, I should imagine that the background experiences more than a thousand changes in place.

These changes may be accomplished at any speed the novelist chooses. Faster than sound, or slower than the actual occurrence of the journey. Hardy begins *The Return of the Native* with an enormous landscape of Egdon Heath, changes (in a mere line; no scene-shifters, no toiling interval, required) to a reddleman's van, later returns swiftly to a huge rolling ascent embracing "hillocks, pits, ridges, acclivities, one behind the other" and covering many miles of heath. Napoleon crosses the Niemen; on the next page of *War and Peace* Boris Drubetskoy is dancing a mazurka at a Moscow ball. In *Far From the Madding Crowd*, on the other hand, Fanny Robin's journey along Casterbridge Highway to the workhouse occupies several thousand words.

The novelist can not only command any weather he

desires for his settings, but can change this weather convincingly—a capacity lacked by every other art. To present a change in weather convincingly by scene, by specific incident alone, requires too great a number of incidents to be worth while; to avoid tedium by reducing the number of incidents is to court naïveté and lack of verisimilitude. Who has not heard the audience titter at a too sudden gale or thunderstorm on stage or film? But these transitions are beautifully accomplished by mingled scene and summary in the novel; English literature, like the English climate, is full of them and they are as natural as our varying sky. The day changes from fine to wet while Lord Miltoun is on the moors in *The Patrician*, changing with it Miltoun's mood and subsequent action; a snowstorm detains Mr. Lockwood at Wuthering Heights; a sudden flood of the Floss drowns Tim and Maggie Tulliver. Throughout English fiction the night is continually falling, weather is continually turning inclement, thus putting the hero or heroine in need of that rescue by his or her opposite number which starts their story.

We have already noted, when dealing with the use of summary, the great power this type of narrative gives to the novelist with regard to time. Multiply the power of space and time together and the novelist's mobility is amazing. On the same page can be presented the hero galloping along a dark road, the interview a week ago in the capital when the important letter he is now delivering was entrusted to him, the reasons why the letter is important, the villains waiting in ambush for him round the corner, the reasons why the letter is important to them, the heroine weeping and praying for the hero in her country home a hundred miles away—and the hero again, thinking of all these things as he gallops along the road through the dark night. And how our feeling for him is deepened by our knowledge of his past happiness and future danger! To speak seriously, the novelist's mobility through time and place is not valuable merely for itself, that is for the variety, truth and richness it adds to a presentation of life, not merely for the increase in scope it confers upon the plot, which it frees from all physical limitations, but also for the psychological effects it may be made to produce. The significance of Napoleon's crossing the Niemen, the reader's awed sense of fate, his excited suspense and alarm, are all heightened by the scene at the Moscow ball where Boris overhears the Tsar's comment. Our sympathy for Thomasin Yeobright is greatly increased when, having left her returning home unmarried in the reddleman's cart, we meet the respectable aunt whom the poor girl will have to face in the next few moments, and learn in advance what her reactions to Thomasin's mishap are likely to be.

Again, the power of presenting both by scene and summary greatly empowers the novelist with respect to characterisation.

The appearance, the past history, the actions, feelings and thoughts, of a character need to be presented, in one way or another, to make the character thoroughly known. The painter and the sculptor contend that they present the mortal envelope in which a human spirit is clothed more vividly and accurately than the novelist. Their contention is true; nevertheless the novelist has one power which they are denied. The artist and the sculptor present a single specific appearance of a person, an appearance symbolic of all, no doubt, but still only one. The novelist's record of his character's appearance, like one's real life memory of the face of a long-known friend, is compound of many specific views. Moreover, the novelist can summarise a gradual change.

The novelist is not especially empowered with regard to the visible actions of his characters. The painting, the statue, present specific physical actions more vividly; the play, the film, can present a selected series of visible actions more vividly, more strikingly, than the novel. But when it comes to those invisible actions we call feelings and thoughts, the novel is immensely more able (as yet) than any other art form to depict them. Feelings and thoughts do not always result in visible action, even that minute physical action known as a change of countenance. A young nurse standing with hanging head, perfectly quiet and still, before a Sister who scolds her, may be experiencing any one of a tremendous range of strong feelings from shame to hate, and yet not reveal any visible reaction at all. The novelist with his words is able to present her feelings, because extremely subtle words—words infinitely subtler, more penetrating, than any outward action—have been invented to describe thoughts and feelings. The novelist who is telling us the story may use any words he wishes—he may, of course, use words which are far too clever and too subtle for the character to use himself. Thus the novelist with his words is able to tell us more about the character than the character knows or could tell himself, more indeed than anybody in the whole novel knows or could tell about that particular person.

He can, too, summarise the long history of the nurse's

feelings caused by the Sister's bullying during several months. When, therefore, George Eliot remarks in *Middlemarch* that it is now her task "to make the new settler Lydgate better known to anyone interested in him than he could possibly be even to those who had seen the most of him since his arrival in Middlemarch," she is stating a profound truth about the novelist's power of characterisation.

Here is a passage from *Adam Bede* in which she describes the feelings of Hetty Sorrel towards Adam:

Hetty had never given Adam any steady encouragement. Even in the moments when she was most conscious of his superiority to her other admirers she had never brought herself to think of accepting him. She liked to feel that this strong, skilful, keen-eyed man was in her power, and would have been indignant if he had shown the least sign of slipping from under the yoke of her coquettish tyranny. . . . But as to marrying Adam, that was a very different affair! There was nothing in the world to tempt her to do that. Her cheeks never grew a shade deeper when his name was mentioned; she felt no thrill when she saw him passing along the causeway by the window. . . . She saw him as he was—a poor man, with old parents to keep, who would not be able, for a long time to come, to give her even such luxuries as she shared in her uncle's house. And Hetty's dreams were all of luxuries. . . . She thought if Adam had been rich and could have given her these things, she loved him well enough to marry him.

Did Hetty know all the complex baseness of her feelings towards Adam? No; nor could she have expressed it if she knew it. Among the other characters her aunt Mrs. Poyser possibly knew it, but could not have ex-

33

pressed it. To express it through scenes, specific incidents, would take many scenes, many pages, and Hetty's feeling for Adam is only one strand in George Eliot's complex story. Only the blend of scene and summary which is fiction narrative enables this subtle analysis of Hetty's mind to be presented in full without limiting narrowly the scope of the novel.

As for the past history of a character: the powers of summary narrative to convey past history have already been discussed and appreciated. Here is part of Lydgate's past, from *Middlemarch:*

He had been left an orphan when he was fresh from a public school. His father, a military man, had made but little provision for three children, and when the boy Tertius asked to have a medical education, it seemed easier to his guardians to grant his request by apprenticing him to a country practitioner than to make any objections on the score of family dignity. He was one of the rarer lads who early get a decided bent and make up their minds that there is something particular in life which they would like to do. . . . He was a quick fellow, and when hot from play, would toss himself in a corner, and in five minutes be deep in any sort of book he could lay his hands on. . . . Something he must read, when he was not riding the pony, or running and hunting, or listening to the talk of men. . . .

He picks up an old Cyclopædia and reads about the valves of the heart.

. . . From that hour Lydgate felt the growth of an intel-lectual passion. . . . Lydgate did not mean to be one of those failures . . . he had a youthful belief in his breadwin-ning work, not to be stifled by that initiation in makeshift called his 'prentice days; and he carried to his studies in

34

London, Edinburgh and Paris, the conviction that the medical profession as it might be was the finest in the world. . . . Lydgate was ambitious above all to contribute towards enlarging the scientific, rational basis of his profession. The more he became interested in special questions of disease, such as the nature of fever or fevers, the more keenly he felt the need for that fundamental knowledge of structure. . . . He did not simply aim at a more genuine kind of practice than was common. He was ambitious of a wider effect; he was fired with the possibility that he might work out the proof of an anatomical conception and make a link in the chain of discovery. . . .

It would be difficult to find an art other than the novel, a medium other than narrative summary, which could present the facts of Lydgate's past life so fully in so short a space.

That the play and the film have their own methods of presenting such facts—soliloquy, dialogue between other characters, the acting of the actor impersonating the character, specific scene and so on—is of course true, but such devices are often lengthy and cumbersome, and at their worst descend to clumsy informatory conversations open to the objection of Sneer in *The Critic* that "there certainly appears no reason why" one of the characters "should be so communicative" to another. That the material suitable for drama and film is not the same material as is suitable for fiction is another true conclusion; all that is claimed here is that fiction narrative provides an admirable medium for presenting character, setting and story.

The narrative medium also gives the novelist a great power of comment on his story if he wishes.

The earlier novelists use the power crudely and freely; theirs is the familiar "gentle reader" technique. Fielding occupies the first chapter of each book of *Tom Jones* in talking directly in his own person to the reader about his story and the people living in it. Scott comments thus directly; so does Thackeray; so do Trollope and George Eliot. Meredith uses direct comments very frequently, both in such harangues to the reader as the prelude to *The Egoist* and the first chapter of *Diana of the Crossways*, and less obviously in scattered but frequent sentences like: "The dead are patient, and we get a certain likeness to them in feeding on it unintermittingly overlong." (*The Egoist.*)

The gradual decline in the use of direct comment, till at last it is heaved overboard with a splash by the twentieth century, is a fascinating study, which should be attempted by a contemporary critic in the interests of that *corpus* of fiction criticism I mentioned in my introduction. Lubbock of course is the prime authority on this gradual elimination of the direct comment, this gradual de-substantiation of the narrative figure on the wall till he is a mere ghost—or, better, a mere medium not allowed to speak for himself but only repeating such fragments as he can catch of what the spirits in the world over the wall utter. But Lubbock, writing in 1921, had not witnessed the final splash of the discarded technique, the final self-denying ordinance of the novelist narrator; in a word, he had not read the later novels of Virginia Woolf or seen the school of fiction which her new methods created. Moreover, lacking the end of the story of the narrator's abdication, he could not see its historical, sociological and psychological implications. To me it seems that these are of great significance. The transition from the robust harangues of Fielding and Trollope to the deliberate refusal of direct comment by the Armistice period novelists—whether you attribute it to an abnegation of authority, a failure in confidence, or the development of a more sophisticated technique, it is the history of the change in the English social attitude. A study of the transition might well illuminate the sociology of two hundred and fifty years of the English world.

But every novelist comments *indirectly*. He can't help it. For he is using words, and his choice of words gives his opinions away. The very adjectives and adverbs, the very nouns, betray him. Consider for example these three sentences:

A smile of triumph played over George's face.
A smirk of triumph played over George's face.
A snarl of triumph played over George's face.

It is clear that the novelist holds different views—and therefore means you to hold different views—of George in those three cases. "Smile" is a non-committal word; whether we shall like George or not depends on what he is smiling about. "Smirk" makes him fatuous, "snarl" hateful. Call a man "mulish" or "unfaltering," call a measure "rash" or "progressive," "reactionary" or "traditional," and the impressions made are worlds apart.

(It is this power of comment, inherent in the novelist's narrative medium, which makes the concealment of the identity of the criminal so difficult in detective stories. Suppose the house-party are arriving for the weekend, and George comes out to greet them. With a smile of welcome. Ambiguous, but on the whole George is probably not the murderer. With a smirk of welcome. Ah, he's either a villain or a fool. With a snarl of welcome. The criminal without a doubt—unless the novelist is not playing fair. If the novelist describes George at all fully, he gives away his own view of George. If he does not describe George, nowadays that makes the sophisticated reader suspicious too. However, this is a digression.)

Even the very position of words, the way they are placed in a sentence, their proximity to other words, reveals their writer's views. For example, in *The Country House*, when Galsworthy is describing George Pendyce taking a morning's shooting, he writes a couple of sentences thus:

In the sunlight the dead bird lay, and a smile of triumph played over George's lips. He was feeling the joy of life.

In that sentence the juxtaposition of the contrasted words "death" and "life" helps to show what Galsworthy thinks of people who shoot pheasants for pleasure.

All this is perhaps merely to say that words express their writer's meaning. My point is that the writer's meaning cannot be kept out of his words. It is nonsense to pretend that the novelist is not there, not sitting on the wall, when all the time, except when the characters are talking, it is the novelist's words that we are hearing. The reader cannot receive a vivid impression of a character's lifting an arm without receiving also an impression of what the novelist thinks about it; for to be vivid, the narration must say how the lifting is done, and the words revealing that "how" will reveal also the writer's comment. Whether this comment should be subtle and indirect or direct and obvious is a matter of taste, of æsthetics.

not morals; that it is present is an inescapable condition of the novelist's work.

If the novelist's power of presenting character is multiplied (as it is in fact) by his power of presenting time and space, and to it is added his power of comment, there becomes visible his tremendous, his almost un-rivalled—I myself believe it quite unrivalled—power, his amazingly extensive scope, in the presentation of life. Because his medium is a fictitious narrative, a blend of summary and scene, the novelist is able to tell us what people did, where they did it, when they did it, how they did it, why they did it, and what the writer thinks about it as well. There is nothing in life—no landscape however vast, no feeling however minute and subtle, no piece of action however lengthy or complex—which a novelist cannot put into his novel, provided only that his talent is equal to the task. (If words already exist to express the selected phenomena, his task is by so much the easier; if not, he can invent them.) Provided only that he has the knowledge and imagination to conceive it, and the capacity to handle the words necessary to write it down, the form of fiction narrative as moulded between 1719 and 1919 allows the novelist to express it freely, powerfully, and without any limitation save his restriction to words.

VIII

CONTEMPORARY TRENDS

WHAT has happened to fiction narrative since 1919? (A somewhat arbitrarily chosen date; 1915 perhaps would be a better one.)

To answer that question requires in the first place a critical textual study of the work of Dorothy Richardson, Virginia Woolf and James Joyce. I can only hope here to hint at the outlines of the discussion which such a study would fill in and illuminate.

Dorothy Richardson in her series of novels (*Pilgrimage*) dealing with the life of a girl Miriam, *as that life passes through Miriam's consciousness*, began, as she says herself, a "fresh pathway," not only in the substance of fiction but also in its technique. I shall never forget the thrill of meeting, in the first of the series (*Pointed Roofs*, 1915) the intense living truth of its presentation of life through what I should now call its "maximum-scene" technique. If the work now seems less exciting in these respects, it is only that the path has become a highway because Dorothy Richardson blazed the track so well.

The lack of a proper critique of fiction narrative at the time led to a good deal of misrepresentation of Dorothy Richardson's achievements and aims. As she says herself:

"Phrases began to appear, formulæ devised to meet the exigencies of literary criticism. 'The Stream of Consciousness' lyrically led the way, to be gladly welcomed by all who could persuade themselves of the possibility of comparing consciousness to a stream." If the new conception of life she presented was but half understood, the technique through which it was presented went unrealised and ignored. It was another writer whose first book also appeared in 1915, Virginia Woolf, who, using the stream of consciousness technique as the vehicle of a brilliant and poetic vision of life, became aware, and made readers everywhere aware, of its divergence from the traditional type of narrative and the reasons for that divergence.

After her first two novels (*The Voyage Out* and *Night and Day*), which are written in the traditional blended narrative form, Mrs. Woolf rejected that ingredient which we have agreed to call summary, called by her description. "I regret to say," she remarks in *Mr. Bennett and Mrs. Brown*, a paper read to the Heretics, Cambridge in 1924, "that I threw that ugly, that clumsy, that incongruous tool out of the window." Her reason for thus throwing summary out—of a porthole, I feel, for the splash was resounding—she gives by saying that if she had employed it: "My Mrs. Brown, that vision to which I cling though I know no way of imparting it to you, would have been dulled and tarnished and vanished for ever." She had already, however, found a way of imparting her vision, and used it in *Jacob's Room* (1922).

It would be helpful at this point if I could descant briefly on the Bergsonian conception of life as an unceasing becoming, an "actual present now" into which the past is gathered as it presses forward like a wave into the future, which is continually becoming actual. But in a letter I had the honour to receive from Virginia Woolf on the subject of some notes I wrote on her work, she stated that she had never read either Bergson or Freud; I must therefore arrive at her view of life and her mode of presenting it as independently of Bergson as she did. A passage in her essay on modern fiction (*Common Reader, I*) puts her intention clearly. "Examine for a moment," she says:

> Examine for a moment an ordinary mind on an ordinary day. The mind receives a myriad impressions . . . from all sides they come, an incessant shower of innumerable atoms. . . . Let us record the atoms as they fall upon the mind in the order in which they fall, let us trace the pattern . . . which each sight or incident scores upon the consciousness.

"Let us record the atoms as they fall upon the mind in the order in which they fall"—let us, that is, record, as Dorothy Richardson did for Miriam, the direct experience, the actual perception, of a single moment in its becoming, for only by so doing shall we present life in all its vivid actuality. Life is not lived in a summary, but in a continual flow of changing single perceptions; therefore the summary is not only "ugly" and "clumsy" but "incongruous," that is, out of keeping with the reality of life. The scene, the presentation of the specific moment, is the only truthful mode of presenting life.

The development of this idea and its accompanying technique in Virginia Woolf's work is of prime importance to English fiction. The technique seems first to present itself in the short sketch called *Kew Gardens*

(1919), which presents an impression of certain specific moments in the life of Kew Gardens one summer afternoon. *The Mark on the Wall* (1919) reveals a slight development. The writer presents herself as sitting by the fire after tea with a cigarette and surveying a mark on the wall. What is this mark? If made by a nail, it must have been to support a miniature—her mind slips to the miniature, to the people who rented the house before her. But perhaps the mark was not made by a nail, perhaps it is—again the principle of association works. In the course of her meditation on this mark, we encounter in Virginia Woolf's mind miniatures, fields of asphodel, a rose leaf, Troy, Shakespeare, Charles the First, personality, the Victorian era, tablecloths, Whitaker's Almanack, tumuli, antiquarians, retired Colonels, plum jam, men of learning, trees, cows, fish—and finally hear that the mark is a snail. We hear, that is, *everything that passes through Virginia Woolf's mind in a few specific moments;* all the atoms that pass through her mind in the order in which they pass. What the writer recalls now is as much part of now as the cigarette she is smoking; thus the past is part of the present and no summary of it is necessary.

In *Jacob's Room* (1922) Virginia Woolf employs this "specific moment" technique for the first time in a novel. She presents the life-story of a young man who was killed in the 1914-1918 war, in a series of brilliant pictures of specific moments in his life. There are no fewer than one hundred and forty-five scenes, separate "specific moments," in this novel. There is not one single linking summary of any kind. Why should there be, contends Virginia Woolf, when all the past is implicit in the present? The intermediate happenings between the scenes

43

will all be there, gathered up into the next specific moment she chooses to render.

In *Mrs. Dalloway* (1925) the presentation of the actual present now is extended by the recording of several simultaneous perceptions of the moment. We are told Clarissa Dalloway's stream of consciousness for one day, all Clarissa thinks, sees, remembers and feels from the moment she sets out to buy flowers for her party to the moment in the evening when the party is over. But we are also told other people's consciousness of some of those moments: Septimus Warren Smith (who is going mad) and his wife Lucrezia; the mental specialist Sir William Bradshaw; Peter Walsh, Clarissa's old flame; Richard her husband; Elizabeth her daughter; Miss Kilman, Elizabeth's governess, and many others. Their perceptions are skilfully linked, not by a connecting narrative summary, but by the objects which they perceive, by their arrival at the same specific moment; there are no chapter divisions, the story constantly breaks off, to begin again at the same moment from another point of view. For example: Clarissa, buying flowers, hears a car backfire outside. The noise is heard by all kinds of people, including the Warren Smiths, whose story is taken up and followed for a while. Later in the day, when Septimus has killed himself, the ambulance comes for him; there is a break in the narrative, then Peter Walsh hears the ambulance bell. *To the Lighthouse* (1927) has in its two main sections the same technique, subtilised and extended: the actual present now of a series of specific moments, with no connecting summaries. The past stories of the characters are revealed through their present stream of thought. The links here are less obvious, more subtle, than those in *Mrs. Dallowy*; the story glides from one person's perception to another, by the route of a subtle associationism. In the middle section of this novel, the beautiful interlude called "Time Passes," there is an interweaving of scene and summary so skilful that the joins are barely discernible.

In *The Waves* Virginia Woolf keeps with the most literal strictness to her own dictum about recording atoms as they fall upon the mind in the order in which they fall. The story of the lives of Bernard, Louis, Neville, Jinny, Rhoda, Susan, never emerges into the external world at all; we are merely told their actual perceptions of the impacts of the falling atoms, at nine different specific moments of their lives. The beautiful wave-interludes which separate these specific moments and indicate the passage of time are themselves narrations of specific actions.

We ought not to regard *The Years* as an intentional experiment, as it is probable that the present form of the book is not what its author planned. Nevertheless, as an adaptation of the specific moment technique to a story of some twenty persons, covering some fifty years, it has great interest as throwing light on the capacity or otherwise of this technique for presenting large-scale fiction. I am bound to record my own view that this novel supports the contention made earlier in this essay, that scene alone is not as competent in handling life *extensively* as scene-plus-summary, though greatly more competent in creating a feeling of intense participation in the reader.

Amongst those who "simultaneously entered" Dorothy Richardson's "fresh pathway," as she observes in her

1938 preface to *Pilgrimage*, were two figures. "One a woman mounted upon a magnificently caparisoned charger, the other a man walking, with eyes devoutly closed, weaving as he went a rich garment of new words wherewith to clothe the antique dark material of his engrossment." The woman is of course Virginia Woolf; the man James Joyce, who carries the recording of the specific moment one step further, since the atoms falling on the mind in *Ulysses* and *Finnegan's Wake* are themselves subdivided into particles, following each other so rapidly that the succeeding particle often blots out its predecessor, causing the recording words to telescope.

There is no doubt that the technique of elimination of summary, of presentation of life through specific moments alone, which in Virginia Woolf's hands yields an effect of brilliant and poetic beauty, in Joyce's a penetration so keen that it reaches the deepest and darkest levels of the mind, has had an immense influence on contemporary English fiction. There is no doubt, either, that this technique represents a divergence from the main traditions of the English novel as established in the last two hundred years. Will fiction written in this technique remain a branch merely, or will the whole tree-trunk bend in that direction? Will it remain a sport or become a species? Or—and this is perhaps both more probable and more desirable—will the brilliant new conception of recording life through moments of consciousness be added to, merged with, the former technique, enriching both?

We are, in any case, infinitely obliged to Virginia Woolf and James Joyce, not only for the great intrinsic merit, the striking originality, of their work, but for making us conscious of the true nature of fiction narrative. Before they wrote—and this is especially true of Virginia Woolf—we did not understand the texture of the fabric the novelist wove; we had not perceived, or at least only imperfectly, the existence, certainly we had not perceived the significance, of scene and summary as elements of the novelist's art. By her exclusive use of, her concentration (whether conscious or unconscious) upon, one of these elements, she has illuminated its possibilities and their limitations.

But need we throw away the summary? To me it seems a highly civilised tool. The child, the savage, the untutored, cannot summarise; they can relate specific instances but not sum or deduce from them. If the novelist has at his command both the specific and the integrated, why should he confine himself to one of these alone? To present a complex piece of action through the specific alone inevitably entails either repetition or gaps; for either in every scene the characters have to remember what has happened since the last scene at inordinate length, or their past is inadequately rendered and their psychology appears incomplete. Why, in our wish to gain depth, should we have to sacrifice extensiveness? The summary is the unique privilege of the novelist; employing both summary and scene, he is able to traverse long actions as rapidly, and one small action as slowly, as he likes, with all the gradations in between. Surely, then, we need and should use both.

That the summary can be and often has been tedious, unlifelike, ill-employed, is true; that it has been used quite unconsciously by novelists ignorant of the proper use of the tool in their hands has been true and is still true today. But to throw the summary away at the very moment when other arts—the film and the broadcast—are just beginning to employ it to intersperse their scenes, seems strange. Such films as *Citizen Kane*, *Double Indemnity* and *The Portrait of Dorian Grey* use brief spoken summary narrative during their scenes to link up the action, and we hail them as masterly examples of new technique; the contemporary broadcast "feature" programme often employs narrative summary in the same way as the novel, for the continual use of heard scene has been found monotonous and uninforming. If summary is useful to film and radio, why should its onlie begetter, the novel, reject it?

IX

CONCLUSION

THE TRUTH is that we know far too little about narrative; our pronouncements are guesses in the dark.

A critical history of the art of narrative, the art of
story-telling, is urgently necessary. This should study
story-telling (whether in verse or prose) from the days
of the Greeks and Romans, through the jongleurs, Boc-
caccio, Malory, Lyly, to the present day. Many interesting points would emerge for investigation. Do certain
nations tend more to summary in their fiction, others to
scene? How can this preference be related to their physical and psychological characteristics? Is the summary,
the scene, or a mixture of both, the later historical development? When did the convention impose itself of
using quotation marks for, and "insetting" dialogue?
What effect has this had upon the art of narrative?
What variations do the practices of oral and written
telling respectively impose upon the art of narrative?
(A story told orally cannot stand many pieces of direct
dialogue, for the narrator's attempt to impersonate his
characters' voices tends to become both ridiculous and
ineffective to the hearer's ear; whereas on the printed
page —dialogue is highly desirable because it breaks up
the monotony of the lines to the reader's eye.) How is

characterisation affected by summary and scene? Do certain writers through the ages tend to prefer summary, others scene? And why?

These are only a few of the questions which rise to the mind. They indicate the rich field to be explored by the critic of the art of narrative.

The present observations, admittedly merely introductory, have been gathered together here in the hope that possibly they may stimulate research into this fine, complex, subtle art.